Introduction

In 1999, the British Methodist Conference enthusiastically received the report 'Planting New Congregations'. In a forty-five minute debate, almost every speaker had a story to tell of his or her own experience of new churches that have been planted.

The new churches being planted across the country are growing at an astonishing rate. It is normal for this sort of new church to double in size in its first two to three years.

The number of new members being added is not enough to overturn the overall declining numbers attending church in Britain. But it is large enough to offer real hope to every church. These new churches are also learning lessons from which the whole Church can benefit.

This study guide is offered to the whole Church in the hope that its stories will help every Christian and every church to discover a new confidence. Decline is not inevitable and those people who do not at present attend church are not indifferent to thinking or speaking about faith. Nor are they unwilling to consider becoming active disciples of Jesus Christ.

The stories in the report and in the case studies are all of real congregations, planted by ordinary people, who caught a vision and dedicated themselves to it.

The questions are intended for use by house-groups or by working groups that are exploring the possibility of beginning a new congregation. They are based on the seven lessons from church planting which form part of the report. This booklet is not intended as a practical guide for those planning a church plant, but rather an exploration of what it means to be church in the 21st century. There is a list of useful resources at the end of the book for those who wish to explore further the possibility of planting a new congregation.

session

1 Servant Ministry

study guide

Evangelism in word alone carries very little credibility. Evangelism that is a visiting or 'hit and run' ministry carries very little credibility. To be effective ministry must be incarnated in its local community. This community may be a geographical community or a network of people linked by common interests. The service offered to a community may be a traditional social action ministry such as a café/counselling centre in an area of urban deprivation; it may be developing a sense of community in a faceless sprawl of new housing through a newsletter or community activities. Sometimes the serving will be through a formal programme, sometimes it will be through an informal network of friendship and on other occasions it will be extended by Christians working in secular community groups.

It may be argued that serving the community in this way should not carry an evangelistic element, but should be done for its own sake. However, it can also be argued that to offer the love of Christ in a practical way without pointing out the source of that love is to make people dependent on us rather than allowing them to enter into the freedom that comes from depending on Christ.

The minister of a rapidly growing church was asked the reason for that growth. He replied: "We find a hurt and heal it. We find a need and meet it."

This may seem rather mercenary, and if our aim is simply to persuade people to attend a new church (or any other one) then our selfishness will soon be revealed. However, if our aim is to help people to become the very best that they can be, then one of the results of that care may well be that those same people discover the love of Christ and become his disciples. Another way of expressing the same strategy might be: "Love people until they ask why and then tell them about the love of Jesus Christ."

In adopting this strategy we are drawing together evangelism and social action in a holistic way. This has been a feature of the mission of the Methodist Church in the past; particularly in the eighteenth century and in the Central Hall movement at the beginning of this century.

This approach also acknowledges a changing understanding of evangelism. Research has shown that for most people, the process of becoming a Christian is a long one which lasts from two to four years. It is also true that most people find a close relationship with a Christian as the single most important reason why they come to faith.[1]

Sadly there are many church members who have no close relationships with people outside the church.

In a church planting situation, particularly one where a team is moving into a new area and there are no existing relationships, it's important to build relationships by serving the community first. In this way we earn the right to speak about the love of God.

This approach to ministry also fulfils a prophetic function as the church demonstrates true community.

When a new church adopts a servant ministry it is offering a glimpse of true community. As we serve one another and the world, we begin to share our lives in a deeper way than most people experience. This is arguably one of the most important contributions that the church can make to society.

[1] Finding Faith Today, John Finney, Bible Society, 1992 chapt 4 pp 36-50

questions

1 **Read Luke 10:25-42** Who is my neighbour?
How do we maintain the right balance between serving Christ and listening to him? (verses 41-42)

2 How do we already serve the community:
a) In formal ways by organising church-based activities?
b) In informal ways as church members' work in other community organisations?
Discuss in small groups, then list all the ways that you serve your community.

3 How can we develop the links between Christian service and the evangelistic and worshipping part of our church's life?
How clear should this link be? Look at your list from the last question and see if there are obvious links which can be developed.

4 What opportunities to serve in our local community can we identify?

5 What is our community?
Is there just one, or do we move in a variety of different communities – where we live, work, play, etc?

6 How can we link our service in the community with prayer (individual and corporate)?

A safe place to enquire about faith

The incredible multiplication of Alpha courses around the country in the last few years together with the growth of 'Emmaus – the way of faith' and 'Disciple' courses has demonstrated that there are a lot of people who are seeking to learn more about the faith. The fact that so many of these courses have an informal small group based approach and combine apologetic and experience gives a clue to the way forward. It is perhaps true that the formal teaching content of these courses (and others like them) is secondary to the fact that Christians are willing to talk openly about their faith in a sharing environment. It is also important that the Christians involved in these groups are willing to take seriously the spiritual experiences of those who are seeking faith – even if they are expressed in language and concepts that we may find unfamiliar and even threatening.

For some people the step from where they are to such a group is too big to make and they are happier with the 'seeker sensitive service' approach. This sort of presentation allows people to come and explore in an anonymous way before committing themselves to finding out more. (See paragraph 5.5 in the Conference Report.)

In sharing faith, there are two distinct components which are important – firstly, explaining what we believe & why and secondly, explaining how the experience of faith has changed our lives.

The first is an 'apologetic' component. In this we are trying to give a reason for what we believe. We may begin with moral or ethical issues or arguments about the existence of God or the divinity of Christ. This may be done in a formal way (such as an alpha course) or in an informal discussion.

The second component is our own religious experience. This will inevitably be subjective, but there is a compelling quality about someone who is able to share how they came to faith and what it means to them to believe.

As relationships develop and trust deepens, the discussion will inevitably turn to the 'seekers' own experiences and the problems that they have either in understanding or in accepting the Christian faith.
In the early church, the process of 'catechesis' or instruction before a new Christian could be baptised would take three years. Recent research has shown that this approach is healthy. For a person to both experience and understand the love of Christ usually takes two to three years.

Most growing churches depend on small groups for the environment in which this sharing can happen. There has been a growing realisation in recent years that the small group is not just a good place for mature Christians to deepen their faith, it is also the best place for enquirers to discover faith. The cell church movement is one which depends on small groups as the basic building block of church and emphasises relationships based on honesty which lead to a growth in Christian maturity. This model is a very flexible one for church planting

Whatever model of faith-sharing we adopt, it is important that our model allows space to ask awkward questions without us appearing either condescending or shocked at what we hear. It is also important to share faith in the context of a deepening relationship where faith is 'caught' as well as 'taught'.

questions

1. **Read John 3:1-18** Is Jesus talking about experience, understanding or both?
   How does Jesus describe the purpose of conversion (verses 3, 5,17)?
   How can you know that you are 'born of the Spirit' (verse 8)?

2. How did you come to faith? Try to tell your own story in two or three minutes.

3. How do we strike the right balance between experience and understanding as we find faith?

4. Try to picture your friends – what would be an appropriate event to introduce them to the Christian faith?
   Does your church provide the right sort of events?

5. What were the key moments in your journey of faith? What helped you to greater understanding of what you believe and/or a greater sense of commitment to Christ and his Church?

6. Try to obtain details of 'Alpha', Emmaus, Disciple and any other basic Christianity courses. Which one is best for your church? If you already do one of them – what comes next? Can you offer a new Christian a two-year exploration of the faith as the early Church did?

3 A search for transcendence

Worship styles in church plants vary a great deal. Perhaps the only common factor is that they are willing to explore new ways of worship in order to be relevant to new groups of people. However, they do all seek to communicate a sense of awe. It is a difficult balance to speak the vernacular of the local community and also to acknowledge that no language can fully communicate the reality of the triune God. Whatever worship style is used, we worship a transcendent God. The sense of otherness of God (often despite a very informal worship style) is an important factor in offering hope. It is important that our worship is directed to a God who understands our culture, and yet who is able to transform both the individual and the culture in which they live. The way in which new congregations express their sense of awe may be very different from that of traditional churches. Indeed, some Christians schooled in traditional ways may find themselves questioning whether what they experience is truly an act of worship. There will always be a tension between seeking to be both relevant and reverent that may result in a loss of the sense of transcendence. Perhaps the best test of this is the reaction of those who come from outside the church. If they sense the presence of God in life-changing ways then the search for transcendence has been successful.

How do we define good worship? One of the easiest ways to begin a controversy in almost any church is to suggest changing worship.

Our theology affects our heads, but worship touches our hearts. However, the majority of the population have voted on our worship with their feet. They are happy to talk about spirituality and faith, but find our worship irrelevant. The church has not been effective at attracting people with no previous church history, but even more worrying is the fact that we seem unable to persuade the children of existing members to continue to attend worship.

Church planting offers an opportunity to try new ways of worshipping without offending those who prefer traditional worship in existing churches. Sometimes this can be achieved by planting a new congregation in an existing building in order to meet the worship needs of a different section of the community (see the case study on the 'Cafe Church' at Raynes Park Methodist Church, page 38).

The hardest question to answer is what style of worship should we offer? Even the new churches (formerly house churches) are facing the same situation as they discover that their young people do not find 'modern' songs by Kendrick, Richards and others modern enough!

Should we try to establish worship services with new music for each new generation? What implications does this have for the technology and musical expertise involved? Many Methodist churches do not yet own an overhead projector, how will they cope with a computer controlled video projector?

This also raises important issues about the nature of church. Is it still possible to be a church which appeals to every generation and a rich diversity of culture?

How do we find a way beyond musical styles and fads to the place where we are worshipping God with all our hearts, minds and souls?

Given the alarming decline in attendance at worship these questions cannot be brushed aside! They are of vital importance for the whole Church.

questions

1 **Read Colossians 3:15-17 and Corinthians 14:26-33a**
Are these descriptions of worship in the early Church different from your experience of worship?
How important is participation in worship?
How can we involve more people?

2 Think of a time when worship was especially meaningful. Why was this so?

3 List the essential ingredients of worship. Try to work out together how those ingredients can be expressed in a way that your non-churchgoing friends would welcome.

4 Try to devise an act of worship without depending on musical instruments, hymn or song books.

5 Is it a good idea to 'aim' worship at a particular group in society (youth, families, pensioners, etc)

6 If we begin a worship service for a particular group, how can we help them to realise that they are part of a wider church? Is the circuit an important asset in this?

Team approach and gift discovery

Methodist church planting teams are generally quite small. It is unusual for teams to be bigger than 10-12 people and they are often smaller. (This contrasts with a typical Anglican team size of 20-25 people.) This has the benefit of enabling the teams to work very closely together and to get to know each other well enough to develop gifts in a way that might not happen in a bigger church. Indeed at least one church plant (Birches Head in the Stoke-on-Trent [Burslem Mission] Circuit) was started because a large church did not have enough opportunities for its members to develop their gifts. They consciously began to look for opportunities and discovered an area where a church plant was needed. They quite deliberately channelled the gifts of a group of their members rather than suffering what sometimes happens in larger churches – members leaving because of a sense of frustration that their gifts appear not to be valued.

One of the great conundrums of church leadership is breaking the 80-20 rule. This rule states that 80% of the work will always be done by 20% of the members. We are often reluctant to ask people to contribute too much when they first join the church, but then wonder why they drift away a short time later because they do not feel involved.

In the early days of a church plant it is relatively easy to involve the whole team. However, it is important to plan early to maintain that level of involvement as people begin to join the fledgling congregation. One of the secrets of the Wesleyan revival in the 18th century was the high expectation placed upon members.

There are a lot of resources available to help in both gift discovery and in equipping disciples. If they are well used, new members will be fully released into ministry and will then become agents of growth. If this equipping does not take place, then the leadership will quickly become overwhelmed by the pastoral load of caring for people who should be caring for one another. The congregation will hit a ceiling (often around 30 people) beyond which it will not grow.

Christian Schwarz, a German researcher analysed the reasons for growth in 1000 churches in 32 countries on 5 continents[2], his findings are:

- .... no factor seems to influence the contentedness of Christians more than whether they are utilising their gifts or not......
- None of the eight quality characteristics showed nearly as much influence on both personal and church life as 'gift oriented ministry'.[3]

A significant factor in the release of gifts in individuals is the amount of energy which is put into ongoing lay training.

Those churches which are people-centred in gift discovery tend to grow in both numbers and quality of life more than those which are programme-centred. A programme centred church waits for a vacancy in its existing activities then looks for a person who will fill the gap.

[2] Natural Church Development Hand book, Christian A Schwarz, (British Church Growth Association, 1996)
[3] ibid, pages 24-5

A people-centred church looks at each individual who joins and asks the question: "What gifts does this person have and how can we use them?"

It is inevitable that such an approach will place demands on each new worshipper that will be too high for some and they will drop out. However, if the demands are leading to a sense of fulfilment, then the benefits of such an approach outweigh the disadvantages.

1 **Read Ephesians 4:11-16**
Can you identify apostles, prophets, evangelists, pastors and teachers in your church?
What job do all these people have in common (verses 12-13)?
How can we ensure that the 'whole body' 'grows and builds itself up in love' (verse 16)

2 Think of a time when you were very fulfilled as a Christian – what gifts were you using and what was the result?

3 What are your gifts? Go around the group taking it in turns to listen as the rest of the group identify your gifts?

4 Try to list the gifts needed in a church planting team. How many people will be needed for those gifts to be present?

5 In a church planting situation, how soon would you encourage new members to use their gifts and become active participants – one month, three months, six months or a year? What would be the time-scale in your church?

5 Pioneer leaders

study guide

A study of the Acts of the Apostles shows that on a number of occasions groups of people led by the Holy Spirit take the church into areas where it had not been before. This is not just a case of geographical expansion, but is also a cultural expansion. In each case this expansion is endorsed by the church's leadership and is encouraged to go further. This does not happen without tension or argument, but there is a sense throughout the book that the best leaders are encouraged continually to move outwards as they share in God's mission. So the deacons appointed to look after the practical needs of the Greek speaking widows reappear as church planters in Samaria.[4] The men of Cyprus and Cyrene go to Antioch and preach the Good News to the gentiles.[5] Paul and Barnabas are sent out by the church at Antioch, going first to share the good news in the synagogues of the diaspora, but are then led to Philippi where there is no synagogue and Athens, the home of Greek philosophical and religious debate.[6] Priscilla and Aquila and later Appollos share in this work because of their special ability to relate to people of other cultures.[7] In each case their mission is recognised and encouraged by the sending church. Peter's experience with Cornelius[8] is part of God preparing him to endorse the gentile ministry of Paul, Barnabas and the teams of apostolic church planters who go from Israel into Asia Minor then on into Europe.

[4] Acts 6:1-6 & 8:1-8 [5] Acts 11:19-24 [6] Acts 13:1-17:34 [7] Acts 18:18-28 [8] Acts 10:1-48

That their mission should break new ground in such an obvious way is inevitable given the radical nature of the message that they carried and the commitment to evangelism that they demonstrated. It is perhaps not so obvious, but equally true, that a similar approach to sharing in God's mission is required today.

Church plants are led in a variety of ways, sometimes by itinerant presbyters, sometimes by ministers in local appointments or members of the diaconal order, often by lay people either paid or volunteer. At the moment there is no concerted national strategy to identify the people who have the particular gifts to work cross-culturally and to train and commission them to this work. One of the results of this is that leaders are often placed under unnecessary pressure, because they are trying to make time for church planting at the same time as fulfilling other demanding ministries, or because they are asked to perform these tasks without adequate training. It is vital that a more deliberate policy of identifying those with cross-cultural abilities and training, releasing and resourcing them for this work is implemented.

The Baptist Union has for some years offered a particular approach to training for presbyteral ministry which acknowledges that the women and men on the course are called to a ministry of word and sacrament, but that their principal area of pastoral care is to those who are at present outside the church. It would seem that this is an appropriate recognition of vocation that is worthy of examination.

At present the implementation of the 'The Making of Ministry' report, the establishing of regional theological resource centres and the appointment of training and development officers offer real opportunities to explore ways in which appropriate training for church planting can be established at a number of different levels.

St Paul would not have made a good pastor for the Jerusalem Church. He would have been a square peg in a round hole who would have caused difficulties for the faithful Christians in Jerusalem and immense frustration to himself. Fortunately he wasn't offered that job! He was sent to be the apostle to the gentiles.

To do that job well, he needed the freedom to do things in a radical way without too much interference. He also needed the endorsement of Peter and the Council of Jerusalem. Although he didn't always appreciate it, he also needed James and the traditionalists who continually reminded him to stay faithful to the gospel as he communicated it in new ways.

The church has not always dealt so sympathetically with its pioneers. John Wesley was pushed out of the Church of England, Hugh Bourne and William Clowes were removed from membership of the Wesleyan Methodist Church and founded the Primitive Methodist Church. Many of us today can think of individuals who were square pegs in traditional churches who could not understand or accommodate their vision for doing things in a new way.

If, however, we can identify people with these gifts, endorse and encourage their ministries whilst helping them to be accountable, we may well see new ways of being church emerging which will be effective in communities which are untouched by traditional churches.

If our church planting does not cause traditional Christians to ask the question, "Is this Church?" then we are probably not being radical enough. The Jerusalem Council in Acts 15 was concerned with the question, "How Jewish do I need to be to be a Christian?" The answer that the Council gave was vague enough to give Paul, Barnabas and the other church-planting apostles room to try new ways of being church that worked in the diverse cultures in which they evangelised.

Sometimes we forget that much of what we love about being Methodists (or any other style of traditional Christian) is not necessarily essential to being a Christian, but is part of our peculiar church culture.

Some Christians do not have the ability to make that sort of cultural jump, and they need not feel guilty about loving their traditional style of church. However, we all need to give our pioneers space to be different and encouragement to develop new ways of being church. This is almost certainly the biggest challenge facing the Methodist Church at the beginning of a new millenium. Can our structures and our attitudes, identify, equip and encourage our pioneers?

1 **Read 2 Corinthians 6:3-13**
Is this a description of 'normal' life for a pioneer?
Is it inevitable that pioneers will be regarded with suspicion by others in the church?
How could they (and we) 'open wide your hearts' (verse 13)?

2 Who do we know with 'pioneering' gifts?
How can we support them?

3 Try to think of distinct groups of people who live within one mile of your church who will only become part of a church if it is a very different one from yours. What sort of person (or group of people) would be needed to share the good news of Jesus Christ with this group?

4 Think of the wider church. How can we as an institution "identify, equip and encourage" pioneers?

5 Try to think of a practical way that you can encourage a pioneer this week – pray for them, speak, telephone, e.mail or write to them with a word of appreciation and encouragement. How can we make this a regular part of our ministry?

6 A sense of expectation

Church planting teams normally have high expectations. These expectations are focused in outward activity. It is tempting for established churches to provide programmes, to which they hope people will come. In a church planting situation, especially one where there is no permanent building, the team work on a 'go' model. This is particularly relevant in the period of planning prior to a public launch of Sunday services when the team has more time to get to know people in their community. Once a Sunday service begins a considerable amount of time and energy is expended in preparing worship, setting out a venue and organising children's work and other activities. This is the time when there is considerable temptation to become inward looking. Providing this temptation is resisted and that mission is given a high priority, growth in numbers, depth of fellowship, Christian maturity and service to the community will be normal. As we have outlined elsewhere, the rate of growth will be affected by the degree of cross-cultural mission involved in the project. It could be said that this level of expectation should be normal within the church, but it is almost always the case that the pressure to maintain programmes and to care pastorally for those within the church makes a consistent outward looking approach to mission difficult.

It is not unusual for a new congregation to double in size very quickly. Where careful research and relationship building has taken place, a planting team of 10 people can expect 30 people to an initial service. Some of these people will decide that the new church is not for them, but to maintain 20 worshippers is normal.

It is then difficult to resist expectations of slow growth taking over! If, however, the new church keeps a high focus on mission and evangelism, it is possible to continue to grow at a rate which is unusual in more established churches. Birches Head in the Stoke-on-Trent (Burslem Mission) circuit began eight years ago with a large team of 30 people. Despite a number of that team returning to the sending church after three years, they now average 130 worshippers and have a membership of 102 – a growth rate of more than 20 percent per year.

If this sort of growth rate is to be sustained, it is vital that the church puts into practice a team ministry approach. Otherwise the increasing pastoral load will stifle the leadership's ability to focus outwards.

Another area where expectation is vital is that of personal faith-sharing. Many observers have commented that the Church in Britain today is extremely hesitant about evangelism, and many individual Christians are not well equipped to talk about their faith.

The cell church movement places a high emphasis on every Christian actively praying for their friends and families. Praying that God will bless them in every way, but especially that they will become disciples of Jesus Christ. People who pray like this often find God challenging them to be part of the answer to their own prayers and become more involved in the lives of those for whom they pray.

questions

1 **Read Ephesians 3:14-21**
What is the foundation of our expectation?
What is the relationship between prayer & expectation (verses 14-16)?
Do we expect for others more or less than we expect for ourselves (verse 18)?

2 What do you expect the membership of your church to be one year from now? Ten years from now?

3 If your answer to question 2 is a reduction in numbers, how can you form a group which expects to grow in your area?

4 Which of your friends, family, and/or work-mates would you like to see becoming a follower of Jesus Christ and a committed member of his church? How can you influence them?

5 Bearing in mind that it takes most people two to three years to make a Christian commitment, how can we and our churches take this sort of pilgrimage seriously?

A sense of risk 7

The incarnation of Christ demonstrates very clearly that God's mission involves vulnerability and the very real prospect of failure. Perhaps the church needs to rediscover this dimension of its mission. It is certainly keenly felt by those who step out in faith to begin a new work. There are no guarantees and even the most careful preparation and training cannot eliminate the element of risk. However, when we are weak we are strong and many church planters have experienced the growth in faith that only comes by risking vulnerability for the sake of the Kingdom of God. At a time when the Methodist Church is facing restrictions on budget and on the allocation of personnel (particularly presbyters), it is vital that we do not concentrate all our resources in maintaining the institution. Now more than ever it is vital to release personnel and finances in a risky way. It is in these risky ventures that the clue to the way forward for the whole church may well be discovered.

A tee-shirt slogan read, "If you're not living on the edge, you're taking up too much room!" Is this a good description of how it feels to be part of your church?

It is an easy temptation to see the Church as the one place that doesn't change in a world where everything else is changing at bewildering speed. However, this is not what we were called to be. One of the hall marks of the early Church was its adaptability in changing cultures.

If the Church today is to fulfill it's mission, it will inevitably mean that many of us who are disciples of Jesus Christ exercise our discipleship in ways which make us feel both vulnerable and inadequate. The much publicised problems of the 'Nine o Clock Service' in Sheffield, serve as a warning as to what can happen if we take too many risks. If we become fearful and take no risks, then our failure may not be as obvious, but it will in the long term be more damaging to the life of the Church.

How do we assess risk properly? When does faith cross the line and become foolishness?
Perhaps the hardest thing to do is to both encourage our pioneers to take risks and at the same time provide the sort of support and encouragement that helps a risk to become a reality!

1 **Read 1 Corinthians 9:16-27**
Paul feels compelled to preach the gospel (verses 16-18) – can you think of times when you felt compelled to do something for God, even though it was risky?
Is Paul 'two-faced' as he tries to communicate the good news in language that his hearers will understand? How does he avoid the danger of changing the content of the gospel as well as its presentation?
Paul not only takes risks, he perseveres until he sees fruit, what is our target and how will we know when we've achieved it?

2 Who do you know that is involved in risky ministry? How can you support them?

3 Can you think of an occasion where you took a risk for the sake of the Kingdom of God? What happened? Was it a good experience?

4 If a church plant does not continue, has it failed? If not, why not?

5 How long should you persevere with a risky venture before accepting failure?

6 Can you think of an opportunity in your area to share the good news of Jesus Christ which would be risky, but potentially a significant advance for the Kingdom of God? Who would be needed to meet this opportunity?

1 Café Church Raynes Park

case study

“We started café church just over two years ago to serve a number of students living in the Wimbledon area who were very loosely attached to the local Methodist church. It was clear that some of them had a real faith, and a sincere need to meet with other Christians for worship and fellowship, but that the ordinary services were not really meeting the need. Their attendance was irregular, their commitment low, and there was a sense of 'duty' about church attendance.

With the active support and enthusiastic practical encouragement of our local minister, Rodney Hill, we drew together a group of these students to begin to pray and talk about planting a new church within our existing building. This first stage of planning and prayer was crucial to the whole experiment. We had to come to some kind of consensus about what we were trying to do, and everyone involved had to really 'own' the idea. A number of key characteristics were identified about the kind of church we wanted to be.”

Rev Rob Frost

Non-institutional

"Sadly, many local churches are so traditional in their language, dress, culture and thinking that they seem unapproachable to many from young and contemporary backgrounds. Modern advertising doesn't so much appeal to linear thinking as to 'gut reactions', and tv commercials don't explore words as much as feelings. The language of film, music, drama and dance is the vernacular of many in contemporary society and if we want to engage in effective evangelism we must learn how to speak it. We decided that we didn't want to offer forms of worship which are cerebral and wordy. We wanted each service to be relevant to people's needs and feelings. We determined that each act of worship would be culturally relevant to the people it was called to serve! So we use a space that looks and feels like a cafe. Smell the baked potatoes, roasted coffee and carrot cake as you walk in. There are no pews, just coffee tables and chairs in small clusters. Low lighting, panpipe music, and a buzz of welcoming conversation."

Spiritually alive

"We decided that our worship would be viewed as a living form like art, and that it would develop in just the same way. Post modernism is a re-discovery of roots, and we decided that café church should give space for traditional liturgy, ancient prayers, the beauty of silence and the flickering aura of candlelight. We decided that we wanted to re-discover the lost art of 'practising the presence of God'. To find a new awareness of the Holy and come to prayer with a new hunger for the Living God. So the evening is unhurried, starting with a leadership prayer-time at half-past six, and opening the café doors at seven. The service rarely ends before nine and often much later. So there's time for conversation, opportunity to 'get into' worship, space for silence, and time to reflect. We don't have to get the whole thing done in under an hour!"

A sense of Community

"We understood that café church should be an antidote to the breakdown of human relationships. It would actively seek to counter the lonely isolation in which countless Londoners live their lives. It would celebrate the contribution of all. Café church would express the Kingdom in real relationships which echo God's adoptive love. It would discover that worship flows from the richness of communal life. Café church would not consist of clubs and meetings but networks of real relationships. Café church would aim to be a village community that would be the focus of deep belonging. It would recognise that the world is not looking for an organisation to join but a community to be part of. That's why a good hour of the evening is spent in conversation. We eat together, drink coffee, and catch up on each other's lives. I enjoy going to café church because it's a whole evening spent with my friends. When I'm down, I know they'll lift me up; when I'm tired, I know they'll pray. I usually come home lifted and renewed. Little wonder then that when we finally turn off the lights at 10pm, many of the group transfer to the pub over the road to continue their conversations!"

Preaching for response

"We encourage the members of café church to preach, and as a result several of them have come 'onto the plan'. It's a safe place to begin, but we actively encourage every preacher to call for response. Café church recognises that the work of preaching is less to do with delivery and style, and more to do with the life of the one who preaches. We actively encourage those who speak to talk about how their faith relates to their working week and to the personal struggles and dilemmas they are facing. After the talk, the preacher invites everyone to tackle some of the points raised in conversation round the tables. The coffee brews again, bibles are brought out, and people from a diverse range of backgrounds with a full commitment to Jesus or practically none, begin to share together."

Using The Arts

"Café church aims to use the arts in its worship, celebration, participation and communication. It must speak the vernacular of the TV generation, and drama is as important than ever. The primary role of drama in café church is not to 'hammer home the message' but to grab the audience's attention, to entertain, to tell stories, to raise questions, to hold up a mirror to human experience and to question people's presuppositions, so that the preacher has a listening audience waiting to make a connection. Several of the team regularly write short sketches on the theme for the evening, and they add a great deal to unpacking the Biblical theme for that night. I sometimes think that it sounds a bit presumptious to call Cafe Church a church plant. Some years ago it might have been considered a youth group or a student fellowship. Yet increasingly it appears to be a kind of 'cell church'. It's not big by any standards. There are only 40 of us after two years. The high turnover of young Londoners means that you have to run in an activity like this to stand still! Nevertheless a number of interesting results of this activity have begun to appear."

1 | New Leaders:

"Undoubtedly café church is identifying, affirming and releasing new leaders into the life of the church. People who several years ago were 'irregular attenders' are now local preachers, running youth groups or kids' clubs or actively involved in leadership in the café church itself."

2 | New Christians:

"Although there are only about five new Christians after two years of activity, that's no mean feat in secular London society. The big advantage of this café-style fellowship is that young professionals are actually likely to invite friends to come along and experience it for themselves. When we visited hundreds of local homes only three people came along to our new café church season. But the influence on those three has been quite staggering. We must do that visitation again."

3 | New members:

"While we don't have 'church membership' at café church, we do encourage attenders to go along to the main services in the church, and to become part of the multiplicity of groups meeting and serving the community on our premises week by week. There's no doubt that some of the café church gang have now become a part of the 'main' church, and are finding their way into the church council and mid-week fellowships."

4 | New hope:

"Finally, however, a word of caution! Don't set out on this without counting the cost. It is very hard work, and sometimes very discouraging. We only operate on 'term times' in ten week seasons. If it ran year round I quite frankly don't think we could do it. None of this could have happened without the active support and encouragement of the local established congregation. They've given space, they've given money, they've given food... and most of all they've given affirmation. Although the clientele of cafe church is largely 20-40' the older folk are always welcome. Several of them have said: 'What an encouragement... so many young people worshipping in our church... and on a Sunday evening!'"

2 The Upper Room, Liverpool

case study

In the days of the New Testament the disciples would meet in the upper room of a house to pray and learn about the ways of God. Earlier this year a team of people from the Liverpool South Methodist Circuit (a collection of methodist churches from the south of Liverpool) decided to follow this example and take the message of God to the upper room of a pub in the city centre of Liverpool and to start a new fellowship there. We felt that there was a real need for people in the town centre to have somewhere they could come and worship in a relaxed and friendly setting and to learn more about God. With this in mind The Upper Room was born.

A team of people mostly from Elm Hall Drive Methodist Church volunteered to go and help run this new church. We held our first service on 20th September 1998. This service was accompanied by a large amount of publicity in the area surrounding Lime Street station – namely the distribution of 4,000 beer mats!! The feedback we received from this has been very positive. In addition to this we were given quite a lot of coverage by the local press, not all of it good, not all of it accurate; but they say there's no such thing as bad publicity. Already we have new members who came for the first time after reading about us in the paper.

On the subject of new members we are very pleased that we are now building our own regular congregation. God has answered prayer in so many ways at The Upper Room and it is exciting to see the way in which people are being reached through what we are doing. As time goes on we hope that this congregation will grow so much we will be forced to the leave the upper room and find a new and bigger venue! Our main goal though is not about how many people we get on a Sunday morning (although the more the merrier!) but to see God's work done and people's lives changed. Services at The Upper Room are hard to describe. We aimed to set up a relaxed atmosphere but when we started we weren't really sure what sort of congregation would turn up, which makes it hard to please everybody!

“We have a lively worship band (as lively as you get after carrying all the equipment up the stairs!) called URBAN D (that's the Upper Room Band for those in the know) who play a selection of worship songs. We have a small army of local preachers who take it turns to deliver God's message. Add to this drama, poetry, contemporary chart music, story telling and other activities and you have some idea of the often chaotic but always enjoyable Upper Room service. While this isn't particularly original we have made one radical step, which causing some preachers a lot of problems – we asked them to limit their sermons to ten minutes!!

Our objective for The Upper Room was to create a church in which people could walk into off the street - or indeed inquisitive drinkers could come upstairs from the bar and immediately know what was going on. So whilst planning it, it made us really look at our church jargon. For example - if someone was to turn up without knowing anything about Christianity the phrase “Jesus please forgive us our sins” raises some questions…"Who is Jesus?", "What are sins?" and "Why do we need to be forgiven of them?". So planning The Upper Room has meant that we have all had to search ourselves for answers.

We've all learned a lot over the church services we've organised. We've learned that some things, like lack of prayer in the service felt wrong, and we've learned that most people do tend to have idea's that they associate with a church service; a reading from the Bible for example, songs and a collection - which we take in a pint glass! God's been generous and faithful to us throughout the preparation and execution of The Upper Room, and it is a project that has seen His involvement throughout.

The Upper Room is aimed at local residents, but since it is in the city centre, a high proportion of residents are students.

I don't know about you, but on Sunday the place I'm off to is the pub to worship…”

Rev David Flavell

3 Cepen Park

case study

"A new housing estate with no church in close proximity and the challenge of Conference to plant a congregation by the year 2000 gave rise to a prayer group based at Sheldon Road Methodist Church in Chippenham, Wiltshire, who focused specifically on seeking God's way forward. Gradually possibilities regarding a Church Plant on Cepen Park South emerged, and eventually a team of people who felt called to this venture began to meet, only one of whom had been part of the original prayer group.

Everyone remained in membership of Methodist churches in the circuit, but began worshipping together in the homes of members of this core group; then moved to the local rugby club which being a bit more spacious, enabled provision of activities for children , and finally to the larger premises of a conference centre attached to the local ambulance station, where the church has now been meeting for two years.

In November 1996 the church changed its status of being a class of Sheldon Road Methodist Church, and was inaugurated as Cepen Park Church (Methodist).

The first aim to become a worshipping community had been achieved. Our other concern was how to serve Cepen Park South, and how to provide a presence actually on the estate. The conference centre has very good facilities, but is a little way from the estate. It is nearer than the churches in the town centre, but is not ideally situated.

Rev Raymond Enticott, the Superintendent Minister looked to the circuit's resources, and with the support of circuit, district and connexion, last summer, 5 Newton Abbott Close was purchased. As significant as having a house in the centre of Cepen Park South was the appointment of a lay worker. Sheila Tonkin moved in during September 1997, and has made the house a meeting place for a carer/toddler group, discussion groups, Alpha and other meetings."

“With a library and quiet room and Sheila's gifts at building bridges into the community, the church has been able to move forward. Morning services try to provide an environment where people new to the life of the church will feel welcomed, with a monthly evening service aimed at providing more time for worship and preaching.

Four times a year the church puts on a presentation in dance, drama, and music in the pub nearest to Cepen Park South. These outreach events are very popular, and have led to people joining Alpha courses, and coming into a personal relationship with Jesus Christ, and into membership.

The church regularly distributes a newsletter throughout the estate, and take time to publicise all its events as fully as possible. Sally Shaw is a Minister in Local Appointment Cepen Park Church. We have an extremely talented music group, and gifted leaders in preaching, teaching, pastoral and youth work who have made so much possible.

It isn't a qualification for attendance, but I think everyone who comes along has a sense of humour that helps oil the wheels of fellowship. This is a young church facing all the challenges that come with the territory of encouraging people to commit, when in many ways that is increasingly difficult with so many other claims made on peoples' lives today. For all that we have seen significant and exciting growth over the last three years.

The dynamic of the church is changing all the time. Mature Christians whom God has called to serve Him there, find that they often have to relinquish what has made them feel safe and comfortable in the past. This is in order to keep the vision of being a church for those outside, very much in mind. This can be extremely demanding, for although our numbers have increased, it will take time before new people will feel able to shoulder the responsibilities of leadership.

Inevitably there are difficulties and challenges, but the church thrives on prayer and love, and we do have the assurance that God is building and growing his people, through the power of the Holy Spirit, in the name of Jesus Christ.”

Rev Sally Shaw

Planting New Churches
Methodist Conference Report, 1999

Background information

The 1992, Conference adopted a report on 'Church Planting': A Way to Growth' in the context of a wider discussion on 'Decline and Growth in Methodism'. The resolutions adopted included the following:

> **2.** *The Conference calls upon every Circuit in the Connexion seriously and prayerfully to consider ways in which God is calling it to growth: to explore in co-operation with its ecumenical partners the possibility of planting at least one new congregation by the year 2000; and to report on its plans to the District Policy Committee.*
>
> **3.** *The Conference encourages every circuit to identify those of its churches where there is evidence of long-term decline, and to report to the District Policy Committee on what action they propose to take.*
>
> **4.** *The Conference directs the Home Mission Division in collaboration with other divisions, to arrange Connexional consultations on church planting as soon as practically possible, and urges each District to ensure it is appropriately and adequately represented.*
>
> **5.** *The Conference directs the Home Mission Division* in consultation with the Property Division and the Ecumenical Committee, to prepare material on different approaches to church planting together with guidelines for circuits wishing to establish new congregations.*

1 Growing New Churches

1.1 To begin a new congregation is to take a step into the unknown. In response to the challenge offered by the Methodist Conference in 1992 for every circuit .... to explore in co-operation with its ecumenical partners the possibility of planting at least one new congregation by the year 2000, a large number of circuits have taken the risk of beginning something new. For the most part, new churches have been started by relatively small groups of people who have been willing to step outside the safety of traditional church structures. They have made considerable sacrifices with no guarantees of success. They have begun new

*now the Mission Education Section

congregations that are quite similar to existing churches, and ones that are radically different. Some have been rewarded with fairly quick growth, others have worked long and hard for small visible returns. What they hold in common is a willingness to take a risk, so that something new may emerge. In the midst of their efforts are signs of hope for the whole Methodist Church. Signs of hope which will only become a real advance if more circuits, churches and individuals are willing to offer themselves in risky service to the world in the cause of the Kingdom of God.

1.2 It is unlikely that there will be one new congregation established in every circuit (689) by the year 2000 (100-120 or almost 20% seems a fair estimate). However, there has been an encouraging response from a large number of circuits. It is difficult to be exact about what has been done because of difficulties both in gathering accurate data and in defining exactly what a new church or congregation is. Indeed tight definitions of what is church seem inappropriate. Some of the new ventures have been easily categorised as new churches; sometimes with new buildings specifically erected for the purpose. Others have been more radical attempts at doing something new which are not so easily recognised as new churches or congregations, but are still trying to incarnate the gospel in a community of faith.

1.3 Some might argue that we already have enough churches. However, to speak of planting new congregations is not just to talk of erecting buildings – it is primarily about building communities of faith which relate well to people in a particular context. If the current decline in Methodist membership is to be slowed, it is vital that as a Church we reach new groups of people in a way that builds faith communities. Some of these may be very like existing churches, others may be very different. But if we do not persuade people to become visible members of the Church, then many of the other good things which we do to establish a Christian presence in the community in non-church ways are threatened because of a lack of resources. Circuits that have responded to the challenge to establish a new congregation have done so in a wide variety of ways. There is no single 'right' way of planting churches.

2 New area, new church

2.1 These have been established in a number of different areas: Local Ecumenical Partnerships in Barnstaple, Gloucester, Derby, York and Swindon. Some meet in homes, others have progressed from homes to temporary accommodation in schools, community centres or portacabins and from temporary accommodation to permanent buildings. They are led by itinerant or local ministers, by deacons or deaconesses and by laypeople. They are established in partnership with Anglican, Baptist, United Reformed and Catholic Christians.

2.2 In Westhoughton, near Bolton, the local churches entered a partnership with the local authority to build a church school that is also a community centre and a church.

2.3 In other areas such as Taunton, Somerset, the Methodist church has taken the lead and established a Methodist church in an area of new housing.

3 New life and vision into old or redundant buildings

3.1 There are a number of circuits which have churches which are either redundant or on the point of closure, but where there is still a need for a visible Christian presence at the heart of the community. In Oldham and in the Medway Towns, a redundant building has been refurbished and a small team from other churches in the circuit have come together to begin a new work in existing premises. Both premises and worship have been made accessible to the local community and the congregations have grown as people who had thought the church irrelevant have been drawn in.

3.2 In Scawthorpe, Doncaster, a Seed Team worked with local Christians to replant a council estate church which was in danger of closure. In Plymouth a redundant Public House has been transformed into a café, advice centre and church serving the needs of a depressed inner-city area.

3.3 In these areas a small team of only 5-10 people can have a huge impact on an area as they come alongside the community in a very real expression of Christian love and sharing. Relatively small amounts of money can also provide huge improvements in a church's ability to fulfil its mission as has been well demonstrated by the 'Vision 2000' scheme operated by the Property Committee.

4 Reaching the places that got left behind

4.1 There are a number of areas of housing which have always been quite a distance from their nearest church building. Individuals may commute to churches a distance away, but others have been discouraged from forming a link with a local church because of transport difficulties.

4.2 In Brinsworth near Sheffield a Seed Team worked with local Methodists and Anglicans to reach a council estate which had churches around it and were able to incarnate Christian community.

4.3 In Dalton-in-Furness all the churches in the town worked together to establish a congregation in a school in part of the town which none of them was able to serve effectively.

5 Reaching new groups of people.

5.1 Sometimes the local churches, despite all their best efforts, are not able to reach particular groups within the community. The differences between the local congregation and other sections of the community are just too large to bridge the gap between them.

5.2 Sometimes there are very different groups of people living in the same geographic neighbourhood whose expressions of worship will be very different. The differences may be the language of the service – new congregations have been planted to help people to worship in Urdu, Chinese and Korean. But language is not the only cultural barrier that must be crossed, although it is one of the easier ones to identify.

5.3 Sometimes the cultural differences are just as great but not so easily defined. A large majority of the population have made the decision (often without a great deal of conscious reflection) that the worshipping life of the local churches is not for them. This does not mean that they are uninterested in spiritual things or without faith. It does mean that they do not perceive the church as offering them relevant help in their spiritual journey. This is especially true among the young. Some churches and circuits have set out to offer a different style of spirituality which may not appeal to traditional church goers, but will effectively reach a group of people who hitherto have had no church affiliation. Sometimes these new congregations will be specifically oriented towards youth. Often they are more oriented towards a wider spectrum of people with services designed to appeal primarily to 'thirty-somethings' hoping that grandparents and children will come too.

5.4 In other places, the worshipping life of the new congregation will also be incarnated in projects that serve the needs of the community. Through this involvement, they seek to provide a diversity of environments in which relationships can be built.

5.5 'The Bridge' in the Hinckley circuit sets out to provide an event that introduces people with little or no church background to the Christian faith. It is run by a group of 35 people drawn from around the circuit who all continue in the lives of their traditional churches as well as giving time to the Bridge. They do not offer a 'service' in the traditional sense, but have a presentation that includes music, drama and teaching. The talk is based on Biblical themes but introduced around an issue which people with no Biblical understanding will identify as relevant. There is little congregational involvement in singing or prayer compared to a traditional service, though both are present. The aim of the presentation is to make it possible for people to come and explore faith without pressure. If they then decide to take the step of committing themselves to the life of the church, nurture and discipling will be provided in a smaller mid-week group rather than on a Sunday.

6 Learning lessons from church plants

6.1 All of these approaches to church planting provide invaluable experience for the whole church. In the discipline of church-planting there is a vital interface between ecclesiology and missiology from which the whole church can learn.

6.2 As church attendance in Britain continues to decline, and the proportion of people who have had no contact with the church for at least two generations grows, it is perhaps a surprise that there are not more questions being asked about what it means to be the church today. Is the perception of many people outside the church true, that Christianity is an irrelevant leftover from an earlier age? Has Christianity anything to say to a post-Christian, post-modern world? Or is it more accurate to say that the particular expression of faith found in many churches today is meaningful to a decreasing number of people, but that it is possible to express the age-old truths of the Christian faith in a more culturally relevant way? Is it possible to live as God's people in the world today so that our faith, and particularly the public expression of faith, will be relevant to more people?

6.3 It is not enough to ask questions about our missiology and how we communicate faith. We must ask the more fundamental question about how we live out our faith in a corporate sense. If the way we live as a church is not in harmony with the way in which we try to relate to the world outside the church, evangelism will never result in mature discipleship. A modern and relevant strategy for evangelism must be earthed in a congregation that meets the needs of the sub-culture that is being evangelised. It is no longer true that one expression of 'church' will meet the diverse needs of a community.

6.4 If we explore these questions in existing churches (as we must), there are huge difficulties. It is difficult to balance the pastoral care of those who find their current expression of faith meaningful and satisfying, with the evangelistic mandate continually to share in God's mission outside the church. If, however, we are able to model new ways of being church where we are less pressured by the needs and demands of a long-established, traditional congregation, then it is easier to assess their usefulness for the whole church. In this way, church planting is one of the movements that can act as a leaven to the whole church. Canon

Robert Warren has likened Church Planting within the established denominations to a tug slowly turning round an ocean-going liner. Its influence is out of proportion to its size.

6.5 As we examine church planting within Methodism, we can identify a lot of new congregations that are very similar to existing churches. The worship or structures may have been fine-tuned for a particular community and a particular expression of church, but they are fundamentally an extension of existing church work. Others (a smaller number) are consciously trying to break with existing patterns and explore new ways of being church.

6.6 The first group should not be discouraged. Research has shown that new churches almost always grow faster than existing churches – particularly in the first five years. It is not unusual for a planting team of ten people to grow into a congregation of twenty to thirty people in the first three years. This would be very unusual in an existing church of the same size. These sorts of churches usually grow by attracting people who have had some previous connection with church but for one reason or another they have ceased to be active worshippers. The establishing of a local congregation with a relevant feel to its worship and ministry persuades them to return to church. These people may eventually have returned to existing churches – particularly at one of the crisis moments in life (starting a family, moving home, grown-up children leaving an 'empty nest', retirement, bereavement etc). The setting up of a new church in their area provides another crisis moment that provokes a decision to attend. At the moment a large majority of the new congregations (of all denominations and streams) are growing by attracting these 'de-churched'[1] believers.

[1] De-churched believers are those who those who once actively belonged to the church. At some point in the past they have stopped attending worship, but have often not lost their faith. (See *Gone but not forgotten*, Philip Richter & Leslie J. Francis, published Dartman Longman & Todd 1998, for a full discussion of this issue). Un-churched people are those who have never had any real contact with the church (See *The faith of the unbeliever,* Martin Robinson, published Monarch 1994).

6.7 This is an important area of mission. However, the group of people with a previous affiliation to the church (like those attending existing congregations) is decreasing within society. As each successive generation has less involvement with the church than the one before, the potential for rekindling an active involvement in church decreases. Perhaps we have not always recognised as clearly as we should the importance of these returning worshippers. Nor have we identified that people who did not attend Sunday School (especially since the collapse in numbers attending Sunday School some 30 years ago) are less likely to bring their own children for baptism or to junior church. In a further generation's time they are also less likely to come back to church at retirement age (as many still do). If contact with these groups has collapsed in the last generation[2], then much of our current evangelism is going to become less and less fruitful as time goes on.

6.8 The group within society that is growing consists of those who have never been part of the church and who do not regard the church as relevant to their spiritual needs. They are not unspiritual or even unchristian, but they are unchurched. If they have already made the decision not to worship in the very many good churches in their neighbourhoods, then it seems unlikely that they will be persuaded to attend a new church that is like them. It is tempting to think that small alterations to the way we worship will make all the difference. We experiment with new songs or musical instruments, new liturgies and increased participation (all of which may be good) but we fail to make any significant impact outside those who already understand church culture.

6.9 The early church had to wrestle with the issue of whether or not it needed to remain Jewish in order to be Christian, and became increasingly separated from the synagogues as time went on. Today we too must wrestle with how we can present the Good News of Jesus Christ in a meaningful way to those who are outside the church culture. This may mean letting go of some cherished traditions in order to express our faith in a more culturally relevant way.

[2] This issue is well illustrated by the Church of England report *All God's Children* published in 1991.

6.10 This problem can not be easily addressed or quickly solved. At its heart is the issue of incarnation. Each community will search for spiritual values in different ways, will explain its spirituality in very different vocabulary and will respond to a servant church in different ways. The experience of church planters has been that the bigger the cultural divide between the evangelist and the community in which they work, the slower will be the process of church planting. It is also true that whilst many Christians can share their faith well within their own culture it is a small number who are able to share faith cross-culturally. In the Acts of the Apostles we see Peter becoming less central to the expansion of the early church because he is so clearly rooted in his own Galilean culture. Paul on the other hand has the ability to work in Jewish, Roman and Greek cultures.

7 Common Themes

As we examine the lessons that have been learnt in recent ventures into church planting there are a number of themes which become clear. If our church planting is to be more effective, we must understand these issues and work out the best ways of communicating them and resourcing them within the wider church family.

7.1 *A servant ministry*

Evangelism in word alone carries very little credibility. Evangelism that is a visiting or 'hit and run' ministry carries very little credibility. To be effective ministry must be incarnated in its local community. This community may be a geographical community or a network of people linked by common interests. The service offered to a community may be a traditional social action ministry such as a café/counselling centre in an area of urban deprivation; it may be developing a sense of community in a faceless sprawl of new housing through a newsletter or community activities. Sometimes the serving will be through a formal programme, sometimes it will be through an informal network of friendship and on other occasions it will be extended by Christians working in secular community groups.

7.1.1 It may be argued that serving the community in this way should not carry an evangelistic element, but should be done for its own sake. However, it can also be argued that to offer the love of Christ in a practical way without pointing out the source of that love is to make people dependent on us rather than allowing them to enter into the freedom that comes from depending on Christ.

7.2 *A safe place to enquire about faith*

The incredible multiplication of Alpha courses around the country in the last few years together with the growth of 'Emmaus – the way of faith' and 'Disciple' courses has demonstrated that there are a lot of people who are seeking to learn more about the faith. The fact that so many of these courses have an informal small group based approach and combine apologetic and experience gives a clue to the way forward. It is perhaps true that the formal teaching content of these courses (and others like them) is secondary to the fact that Christians are willing to talk openly about their faith in a sharing environment. It is also important that the Christians involved in these groups are willing to take seriously the spiritual experiences of those who are seeking faith – even if they are expressed in language and concepts that we may find unfamiliar and even threatening.

7.2.1 For some people the step from where they are to such a group is too big to make and they are happier with the 'seeker sensitive service' approach. This sort of presentation allows people to come and explore in an anonymous way before committing themselves to finding out more. (See paragraph 5.5 above)

7.3 *A search for transcendence*

Worship styles in church plants vary a great deal. Perhaps the only common factor is that they are willing to explore new ways of worship in order to be relevant to new groups of people. However, they do all seek to communicate a sense of awe. It is a difficult balance to speak the vernacular of the local community and also to acknowledge that no language can fully communicate the reality of the triune God. Whatever worship style is used, we worship a transcendent God. The sense of otherness of God (often despite a very informal worship style) is an important factor in offering hope. It is important that our worship is directed to a God who understands our culture, and yet who is able to transform both the individual and the culture in which they live. The way in which new congregations express their sense of awe may be very different from that of traditional churches. Indeed, some Christians schooled in traditional ways may find themselves questioning whether what they experience is truly an act of worship. There will always be a tension between seeking to be both relevant and reverent that may result in a loss of the sense of transcendence. Perhaps the best test of this is the reaction of those who come from outside the church. If they sense the presence of God in life-changing ways then the search for transcendence has been successful.

7.4 *A dependency on a team approach and gift discovery*

Methodist church planting teams are generally quite small. It is unusual for teams to be bigger than 10-12 people and they are often smaller. (This contrasts with a typical Anglican team size of 20-25 people.) This has the benefit of enabling the teams to work very closely together and to get to know each other well enough to develop gifts in a way that might not happen in a bigger church. Indeed at least one church plant (Birches Head in the Stoke-on-Trent [Burslem Mission] Circuit) was started because a large church did not have enough opportunities for its members to develop their gifts. They consciously began to look for opportunities and discovered an area where a church plant was needed. They quite deliberately channelled the gifts of a group of their members rather than suffering what sometimes happens in larger churches – members leaving because of a sense of frustration that their gifts appear not to be valued.

7.5 *Pioneer leadership*

A study of the Acts of the Apostles shows that on a number of occasions groups of people led by the Holy Spirit take the church into areas where it had not been before. This is not just a case of geographical expansion, but is also a cultural expansion. In each case this expansion is endorsed by the church's leadership and is encouraged to go further. This does not happen without tension or argument, but there is a sense throughout the book that the best leaders are encouraged continually to move outwards as they share in God's mission. So the deacons appointed to look after the practical needs of the Greek speaking widows reappear as church planters in Samaria[3]. The men of Cyprus and Cyrene go to Antioch and preach the Good News to the gentiles[4]. Paul and Barnabas are sent out by the church at Antioch, going first to share the good news in the synagogues of the diaspora, but are then led to Philippi where there is no synagogue and Athens, the home of Greek philosophical and religious debate[5]. Priscilla and Aquila and later Apollos share in this work because of their special ability to relate to people of other cultures[6]. In each case their mission is recognised and encouraged by the sending church. Peter's experience with Cornelius[7] is part of God preparing him to endorse the gentile ministry of Paul, Barnabas and the teams of apostolic church planters who go from Israel into Asia Minor then on into Europe.

7.5.1 That their mission should break new ground in such an obvious way is inevitable given the radical nature of the message that they carried and the commitment to evangelism that they demonstrated. It is perhaps not so obvious, but equally true, that a similar approach to sharing in God's mission is required today.

7.5.2 Church plants are led in a variety of ways, sometimes by itinerant presbyters, sometimes by ministers in local appointments or members of the diaconal order, often by lay people either paid or volunteer. At the moment there is no concerted national strategy to identify the people who have the particular gifts to work cross-culturally and to train and commission them to this work. One of the results of this is that leaders are often placed under unnecessary pressure, because they are trying to make time for church planting at the same time as fulfilling other demanding ministries, or because they are asked to perform these tasks without adequate training. It is vital that a more deliberate policy of identifying those with cross-cultural abilities and training, releasing and resourcing them for this work is implemented.

[3] Acts 6:1-6 & 8:1-8 [4] Acts 11:19-24 [5] Acts 13:1-17:34 [6] Acts 18:18-28 [7] Acts 10:1-48

7.5.3 The Baptist Union has for some years offered a particular approach to training for presbyteral ministry which acknowledges that the women and men on the course are called to a ministry of word and sacrament, but that their principal area of pastoral care is to those who are at present outside the church. It would seem that this is an appropriate recognition of vocation that is worthy of examination.

7.5.4 At present the implementation of the 'The Making of Ministry' report, the establishing of regional theological resource centres and the appointment of training and development officers offer real opportunities to explore ways in which appropriate training for church planting can be established at a number of different levels.

7.6 *A sense of expectation*

Church planting teams normally have high expectations. These expectations are focussed in outward activity. It is tempting for established churches to provide programmes, to which they hope people will come. In a church planting situation, especially one where there is no permanent building, the team work on a 'go' model. This is particularly relevant in the period of planning prior to a public launch of Sunday services when the team has more time to get to know people in their community. Once a Sunday service begins a considerable amount of time and energy is expended in preparing worship, setting out a venue and organising children's work and other activities. This is the time when there is considerable temptation to become inward looking. Providing this temptation is resisted and that mission is given a high priority, growth in numbers, depth of fellowship, Christian maturity and service to the community will be normal. As we have outlined elsewhere, the rate of growth will be affected by the degree of cross-cultural mission involved in the project. It could be said that this level of expectation should be normal within the church, but it is almost always the case that the pressure to maintain programmes and to care pastorally for those within the church makes a consistent outward looking approach to mission difficult.

7.7 *A sense of risk*

The incarnation of Christ demonstrates very clearly that God's mission involves vulnerability and the very real prospect of failure. Perhaps the church needs to rediscover this dimension of its mission. It is certainly keenly felt by those who step out in faith to begin a new work. There are no guarantees and even the most careful preparation and training cannot eliminate the element of risk. However, when we are weak we are strong and many church planters have experienced the growth in faith that only comes by risking vulnerability for the sake of the Kingdom of God. At a time when the Methodist Church is facing restrictions on budget and on the allocation of personnel (particularly presbyters), it is vital that we do not concentrate all our resources in maintaining the institution. Now more than ever it is vital to release personnel and finances in a risky way. It is in these risky ventures that the clue to the way forward for the whole church may well be discovered.

Resolutions

- The Conference receives the report and commends it to Circuits and Churches for discussion.

- The Conference affirms the work of those circuits that have planted new congregations as an important contribution to the Church's mission. It further encourages every circuit in co-operation with ecumenical partners to explore the possibility of planting at least one new congregation.

- The Conference affirms the importance of pioneer ministries within the life of the church and directs the Church Planting Steering Group to explore, with other members of the Connexional Team, how training for this work can best be carried out.

- The Conference directs the Church Planting Steering Group in collaboration with other members of the Connexional team and the theological resource centres to ensure that appropriate resources for Church Planting are provided.

Resources for Church Planting

A selected list from the huge amount of literature which is available

METHODIST RESOURCES

Planting New Congregations
Rev Graham Horsley
A practical guide with lots of useful information for circuits and churches beginning to plan a church plant.

Stopping the Rot – Planting New Congregations
A 28 minute video looking at the experience of five new congregations. It is accompanied by three sessions of study material. Using the experiences of those who planned the new congregations and those who joined, it draws out lessons about how to have an effective mission as a church

BOOKLETS

Church Planting: Models for Mission in the Church of England
Bob Hopkins - Grove
Two volumes (4&8) which give an excellent introduction to the subject from Biblical and practical perspectives. Written for an Anglican readership but useful for a much wider audience.

WORK BOOKS

Enabling Church Planting
Bob Hopkins & Richard White - CPAS
A five session course which concentrates on preparing to plant a new church. A very good resource to use for a church planting team at the beginning of their preparations.

Church Planting – The Training Manual
Martin Robinson & David Spriggs - Lynx
A much more in depth book aimed at church plant leaders. It offers a very thorough grounding in the subject.